HOW TO
FRESHWATER
FISH LIKE A PRO

JEFF BURLINGAME

Library of Congress Cataloging-in-Publication Data

Burlingame, Jeff, author.
   How to freshwater fish like a pro / Jeff Burlingame.
     pages cm. — (Outdoor sports skills)
   Summary: "In this 'How-to' guide, learn the basic skills and essentials of freshwater fishing including
     where to fish, what supplies to bring, and how to have a safe and fun trip"—Provided by
     publisher.
   Audience: Grades 4 to 6.
   Includes bibliographical references and index.
   ISBN 978-1-62285-224-6
   1. Fishing--Juvenile literature. 2. Freshwater fishes—Juvenile literature. 3. Fishing--Equipment and
   supplies--Juvenile literature. I. Title.
SH445.B87 2015
799.1'1—dc23
                   2014003718

Future editions:
Paperback ISBN: 978-1-62285-235-2   Single-User PDF ISBN: 978-1-62285-237-6
EPUB ISBN: 978-1-62285-236-9   Multi-User PDF ISBN: 978-1-62285-238-3

Printed in the United States of America
052014 Lake Book Manufacturing, Inc., Melrose Park, IL
10 9 8 7 6 5 4 3 2 1

To Our Readers: We have done our best to make sure all Internet addresses in this book were active
and appropriate when we went to press. However, the author and the publisher have no control over
and assume no liability for the material available on those Internet sites or on other Web sites they may
link to. Any comments or suggestions can be sent by e-mail to comments@speedingstar.com or to the
address below:

Speeding Star
Box 398, 40 Industrial Road
Berkeley Heights, NJ 07922
USA
www.speedingstar.com

Illustration Credits: Shutterstock.com: (©Lou Oates, p. 5; ©Melissa King, p. 6; ©Mr Patrick Morrow,
p. 7; ©JonMilnes, p. 8; ©Fabien Monteil, p. 11(top); ©DoctorKan, p. 11(bottom); ©Samo Trebizan, p. 12;
©Golden Pixels LLC, p. 14; ©graphicsp, p. 17; ©Steve Brigman, p. 20; ©Jeffrey J Coleman, p. 23; ©TSpider,
p. 25; © Peter Zacher, p. 26; ©Kathryn Dyellalova, p. 28; ©Little Moon, p. 32; ©filmfoto, p. 38; ©antpkr,
p. 42; ©Zhelyshev, p. 43; ©Val Thoermer, p. 45); ©Thinkstock: (Mike Watson Images/moodboard, pp. 4, 30;
nickrlake/iStock, p. 21; Fedor Kondratenko/iStock, p. 31; JupiterimagesCollection/Stockbyte, p. 33; Johan
MAllerberg/iStock, p. 37.)

Cover Illustration: ©Thinkstock: Mike Powell/Valueline

CONTENTS

FUNDAMENTALS

Your alarm clock goes off at four o'clock in the morning and you wake to the sound of Dad rustling in the garage.

After taking a second to wipe the sleep from your eyes (and wonder if agreeing to get up so early on a Saturday was a good idea), your enthusiasm takes over and you spring from your bed. Sure, the lights are off in the rest of the houses in your neighborhood and most of your friends won't be awake for hours. But they don't love freshwater fishing as much as you do. You really can't pinpoint why.

Once you get dressed, you head out to join Dad in the garage. You can see that he obviously has been awake a little longer than you have; Dad's almost ready to hit the road. So, after you help him load the last

If your fishing partner is standing with fishing pole in hand, you better hurry up and get ready!

Once everyone is dressed and the car is all packed up, it's time to hit the road and get to a fishing spot.

of the gear into the car, you hop in the passenger's seat and that is what the two of you do. It will be daybreak in less than an hour, and you know from experience that daybreak is the best time of the day to catch fish at your favorite spot. It is a forty-five-minute car ride to get there.

A POPULAR SPORT

Although it may feel like it the moment you arrive at the empty parking lot of your preferred lake, river, pond, or stream, you and your dad definitely are not the only people fishing today. Fishing is, in fact, one of the most popular sports in the United States. More people fish than jog, golf, play football, or ski. Tens of millions of Americans go fishing each year. Some fish so they can help feed their families. Others enjoy the challenge of the sport and spending quality time with family and friends in a relaxing outdoor environment. Whether or not you catch anything on your

"The early bird catches the worm." Beat everyone to the water to start fishing to have the best chance to catch some fish!

adventure (of course you sure hope you do!), freshwater fishing allows you to create priceless memories with a loved one and experience an activity that has been around tens of thousands of years.

HISTORY OF FISHING

In its simplest form, fishing is the art of catching fish. Exactly how, where, and when someone fishes can vary greatly. Artifacts have been found that show humans fished as far back as fifty thousand years ago. And many historians believe fishing was around long before that.

In some parts of the world, a wooden spear is still the preferred fishing gear of choice.

During fishing's earliest days, people mostly used wooden spears to catch fish. Fish were so plentiful that it was easy to catch fish that way. An angler would simply stand over (and typically in) a body of water, wait for a school of fish to swim by, and stab one of them with the end of the spear. The activity was not done simply for sport. Fish were the main source of food for many people during that time, and without it they may not have survived.

As humans evolved, so did the sport of fishing. Hooks—J-shaped tools made of bone, wood, shells,

Fishing began with a wooden spear, and over time, spear fishing has become a sport in itself.

stone, or, later, metal—became popular some twenty thousand years ago. Hooks were also known as "angles," and thus the sport of fishing also became known as "angling."

Anglers tied whatever hook they used to some sort of line. In the earliest days, that line was made of whatever strong substance could be found, such as braided horse hair or silk. The hook and line were then attached to a rod made of bamboo or other type of lightweight wood. Bait was attached to the end of the hook and the bait and hook were tossed into the water to lure the fish to bite. When the fish took the bait, it was also snared by the hook. The anglers then drug the fish back to shore for keeping.

Today, more modern equipment is used in freshwater fishing, but the basics of the sport remain the same as they were tens of thousands of years ago: you find a site where you believe (or, better yet, *know*) there are fish and you go there to try to catch them.

SALTWATER FISHING VS. FRESHWATER FISHING

There are two basic fishing categories. The first, saltwater fishing, is exactly what it sounds like. Saltwater fishing that takes place in saltwater, or water that is in or connected to the ocean. More than 70 percent of the earth's surface is covered by water and 97 percent of that water is saltwater. The oceans are the first body of water that comes to mind when saltwater is mentioned, but there are other saltwater bodies, as well. Seas are one of those, as are gulfs, bays, fjords, sounds, and coastal marshes.

Although most of the water on earth is saltwater, the opportunity to go saltwater fishing is limited for many people simply because they do not live anywhere near a saltwater body. Saltwater fishing also can be more difficult to do because it often involves bigger fish, and oftentimes a boat is necessary to travel to the spots where the fish are. Examples of saltwater fish include flounder, cod, tuna, swordfish, snapper, salmon, and mackerel.

The second fishing category, freshwater fishing, is by far the most popular category of fishing in the United States. That is mostly because it is easier to freshwater fish. And, although there is far less freshwater on the earth than there is saltwater, freshwater sources are surprisingly more conveniently located for most people. Freshwater sources include rivers, lakes, streams, ponds, swamps, and creeks. Freshwater bodies can be found all across the country.

The types of fish that can be found in freshwater sources also are typically smaller than those found in saltwater. According to the popular Web site *Take Me Fishing*, some 40 percent of all the fish on the earth are freshwater fish. Those fish include perch, trout, walleye, pike, bluegill, catfish, and bass. The smaller fish makes it easier, in general, for younger kids to take part in the sport without much adult assistance.

DID YOU KNOW?

Fish cannot see anything below their heads, but they have an extremely wide range of peripheral vision.

Catching bigger fish, like the snapper shown in the top picture, is a thrill some enjoy when saltwater fishing. Yet some big fish like the pike, shown on the right, can be caught while freshwater fishing.

PRO TIPS AND TRICKS

When fishing in a lake or river, find the point where the water goes from shallow to deep. When fish are hungry and scavenging for food, they usually look in this area.

WHY WE FISH

The vast majority of Americans who fish do so recreationally. Recreational fishing is the catching of fish for personal consumption or for sport. Sport fishers sometimes eat the fish they catch and sometimes they release the fish back into the water in a way that doesn't harm the fish. The latter is called catch-and-release fishing.

Those who sport fish do so for a variety of reasons. The Virginia Department of Game and Inland Fisheries believes people fish for:

- **Stress relief.** Fishing allows people to spend time in a setting different than the one they spend their everyday lives in. "Nothing brings on the sense of being alive and helps to rebuild our personal reserves like a day spent interacting with nature," the department says.

- **Social bonding.** Fishing helps strengthen relationships with family and friends.

- **Health benefits.** Being active outdoors helps burn calories and raises the quality of life.

- **Recreation.** "The most common reason you will find with people who like to fish is that it is simply fun," the department says.

- **The thrill.** "Fishing has a way of fulfilling an age-old need of pursuing and catching," the department says. "The thrill lies in the challenge ..."

PRO TIPS AND TRICKS

It's no secret that when it is hot outside, people wish it was cooler out, so why would fish be any different? When it starts to get hotter outside, fish will retreat to deeper waters where it is not as warm.

Fishing can be used as a great time to bond with family.

Of course, those are just a few of the countless reasons people love to go freshwater fishing. American author Henry David Thoreau believed that those who fish aren't really after the fish themselves but after the *experience* fishing provides them. Thoreau believed that to be true on a spiritual level. On a practical level, however, those who go fishing want to catch something. Learning the basics of fishing is the crucial first step in becoming a successful freshwater angler.

WHERE TO FISH

As simple as it may seem, freshwater fishing is not effortless. Winning at the sport takes a lot of knowledge and skill. You cannot simply randomly select any river or lake, show up whenever you would like, and expect to be successful. Knowing where and when to go freshwater fishing is important and will greatly increase your chances of catching fish.

KNOWING THE RULES

Perhaps the most crucial aspect of fishing has to do with knowing the sport's rules and regulations. Just as your favorite professional sports teams have seasons in which they compete, there are seasons in which you are allowed to fish, too. Those seasons vary widely from location to location.

In some locations, it is OK to fish year-round for certain species of fish. In other areas, fishing seasons are restricted. It is illegal to fish out of season. In some areas, it is also illegal to keep what you catch. In those areas, fishers may only practice catch and release. Breaking the rules of the sport can result in some hefty fines.

The best way to determine the seasons in your area is to ask someone familiar with them. Another good way is to contact the agency in your state that is in charge of setting the fishing rules and regulations.

Knowledgeable friends or family members (or maybe even the friendly folks at the state agency) also may be able to give you some pointers, such as at what point of the season you will have the best chance of catching what fish or which locations have been "hot" and which ones have been "cold."

WHERE SHOULD YOU GO?

Lakes. Ponds. Streams. Rivers. All four may be considered freshwater bodies and all four have the ability to support lively fish populations. But that does not mean you approach all four bodies of water the same way when you are fishing them.

Don't do the crime if you can't pay the fine. And in some areas, the fine could be around five hundred dollars!

DID YOU KNOW?

According to the American Sportfishing Association, three out of every four people who fish only do so in freshwater.

Each body of water contains different ecosystems and different places where fish like to hang out. In general, according to the *Take Me Fishing* Web site, "you should always fish in and around structure," when fishing still-water lakes and ponds.

"Structure," according to the site, includes:

- Cliffs and steep shore banks
- Rocks
- Weed beds
- Islands and sandbars
- Fishing holes
- Lily pads
- Piers, docks, and pilings

The sometimes rapid-moving waters of streams and rivers present a different set of challenges than do lakes

PRO TIPS AND TRICKS

Wash your hands. Fish have a remarkably good sense of smell. A body of water with less than .05% salinity is considered a body of freshwater. With less salt in the water, fish can smell the bait much clearer, so it is important to keep any unnatural smells off of the bait.

and ponds. Fish in streams and rivers, according to *Take Me Fishing*, most often can be found in:

- Outside bends of the river
- Rock and boulder pockets
- Eddies
- Drop-offs
- Under overhanging trees and bushes
- At the bottom of dams and falls
- In spring holes

Some freshwater locations may contain only one species of fish, while others may contain several. Even if two fish species share the same water, that doesn't mean they can be caught in the same manner. Different species may prefer to frequent different parts of the same freshwater. Have you ever taken a look at a fish tank that is full of different types of fish? Some prefer to stay near the bottom of the tank, while others may always be hanging out near the top of the water, or underneath the plastic house or tree. The same theory holds true for fish that are taken for sport.

Largemouth bass, for example, prefer water that is quiet, shallow, and has lots of shelter. River trout, in contrast, typically hang out where the food is. This includes underneath trees insects fall off of and into the water, and also in areas where there is some steady current that can float the food to them. Lake trout, on the other hand, live where there is little to no current, so these fish generally move around a lot more than do river trout.

The name is aptly descriptive. Largemouth bass do in fact have large mouths.

During summer months, fishing at dusk is pleasant because the air temperature will cool down significantly.

TIME OF DAY

The time of day you fish also is important. Fishing when fish are most active gives you the best chance of catching something. Exactly what time of day that is depends on the time of year.

In spring, mid-afternoon to dusk is generally the best time to fish, whereas in the summer, early evening to sunset is considered the best time. But even these basic guidelines can change depending on the weather and the location. There are many fishers who even use the phases of the moon as their guide as to when to fish and when not to.

FISHING EQUIPMENT

A quick trip into any sporting goods store reveals aisle upon aisle of fishing supplies. Some poles maybe twice as long as you are tall. Some may be shorter than you. Some fishing line is light blue and some is silver, green, and yellow. Hooks can be single-, double-, or triple-pronged. Bait can be live (squiggly earthworms, anyone?), frozen, or artificial.

Shopping for fishing supplies, also known as tackle, can be one of the most fun aspects of learning how to fish. But it also can be the most daunting. Determining exactly what to buy to take with you on that first fishing trip can be confusing. But by doing a little homework, you can enter that megastore feeling confident that you will be able to find what you are looking for with little trouble.

PRO TIPS AND TRICKS

Each body of water offers its own advantages when it comes to fishing. When fishing in a river, wearing a pair of polarized glasses can be very beneficial to an angler. Its a lot easier fishing in an area where you are able to visibly see the fish you are going after.

Make a list of things needed before entering a sporting goods store. Otherwise the amount of available tackle can cause confusion.

KEEPING IT LEGAL

The most important purchase you will need to make before you go freshwater fishing is a license. At what age you need to get a license depends on which state you live in. In Washington, for example, those ages fifteen and older must have a license to fish. But you can fish for free from birth through age fourteen. In Texas, children don't need a license until they turn seventeen. Check with your state's fisheries department to determine the rules for your area. You also can purchase your license through the department, online, or at many sporting goods stores and other retail locations.

RODS

Fishing rods, also called poles, are a necessary piece of equipment and the basis of your whole setup. There are two main types of freshwater rods: baitcasting and spinning. A baitcasting rod is one in which the reel and line are situated on top of the pole. A spinning rod, on the other hand, is designed so the reel and line are on the bottom of the pole. Most beginners find spinning rods easiest to use.

There are other kinds of rods, as well, including telescopic rods that collapse into themselves for easy carrying when they are not in use, and fly-casting rods used for fly-fishing.

Rods come in various lengths, weights, and strengths, and can be made from several different materials, including graphite, fiberglass, and composites. If you're not sure which one is right for you, ask an expert or a family member familiar with fishing in the area you will be visiting. It may be that a combination rod—one you can buy with the reel and line already attached—will be the best for you to begin with until you get the hang of the sport.

REELS

The easiest of the three basic types of reels to learn to use is called a spincast. Most of the

The most common fishing reel used is the spinning reel.

components of the reel are covered and the line comes out of a small hole at the top of the reel. Spincast reels operate with the simple push of a button with your thumb.

Baitcasting reels sit on top of baitcasting poles and also operate with the push of the thumb on a button. But the spools of baitcasting reels turn when casting, making them more difficult to operate.

Spinning reels are by far the most common reels used by beginning and intermediate anglers. They operate with the flip of a metal bar, called a bail. Spinning reels work well in a variety of fishing environments.

LINE

Selecting the best fishing line for the type of fishing you plan to do is a fairly straightforward task. Although the fishing-line section of sporting goods stores can appear overwhelming, it really isn't that difficult to navigate.

It is most important to know that fishing line is classified by something called "pound-test," the amount of force the line can hold before it breaks. In general, the bigger the fish you are going after, the higher you want the line's pound-test to be. Other choices you will have to make when selecting fishing line include:

Choosing the right weight fishing line and tackle is an important element when fishing.

- **Type of material the line is made from**. Common materials include monofilament, cofilament, braided, fluorocarbon, and fusion.

- **Color**. Fishing line comes in many colors, including clear, blue, coffee, gold, and green. The different colors of line allow you to adjust the visibility of your line in the water. There are times where you might want a highly visible line and other times when you may want your line to be invisible.

- **Diameter**. This is what determines the line's pound-test. There are pros and cons to both thick and thin lines.

TERMINAL TACKLE

Gear that is located at the end of the fishing line is called terminal tackle. Choosing your terminal tackle can be one of the most fun parts of fishing. After you buy it, you should neatly organize it in a tackle box that you will carry with you on your fishing trip. Terminal tackle includes:

- Swivels, which help keep you line from twisting and tangling;

- Bobbers, which are small floats which help keep your hook at a certain depth in the water;

- Hooks;

- Sinkers (weights);

Having a tackle box when fishing is extremely important because it holds all of the equipment necessary for a successful day. It can hold everything from extra lures to back up reels and extra line.

- Lures, which are artificial bait that attract fish with the way their color and by the way the move. Popular lures include flies, jigs, plugs, and spoons;

- Live bait, including crickets, maggots, minnows, and worms.

MISCELLANEOUS GEAR

There is what seems like an unlimited amount of gear being marketed to freshwater fishers. Gear that can be helpful but isn't necessary includes such items as polarized glasses which take the glare off the water; pliers for removing the hook from the fish's mouth after it is caught; a stringer and/or a cooler for holding your catch; insect repellent; a tackle box; rain gear; a boat; and personal food and drink.

In many states, a catch record card is also required for every angler, even those who don't need to buy a license. This is a form that needs to be filled out each time you fish and mailed to the state once a year so it can monitor fish populations.

PRO TIPS AND TRICKS

Who doesn't love a free meal?! Fish love food that involves no effort just like anyone else. So if fishing in an area where there are a lot of ducks, take the hint that there is probably food there. Especially if there are people feeding the ducks, there are going to be fish waiting underneath for food to drop. So if you see a bunch of ducks near one another, cast a line and watch what happens.

It is not as glamorous as shopping for your gear. It is not nearly as fun as figuring out where you are going to go. And it ranks far below the act of fishing itself on the fun meter. But that doesn't mean you can skip learning about how to fish safely. Talking about fishing safety may not be fun, but it is without a doubt the most important part of the fishing puzzle.

To make learning how to fish more fun, it's best to do it with someone that can make it a fun experience.

HANDLING YOUR ROD AND TACKLE

Have you ever been jabbed with a sharp fishing hook? If you fish long enough, you will be—several times and in several different parts of the body. If there are other people fishing near you, they also are in danger of being

DID YOU KNOW?

Fish use bones in their heads called otoliths to hear. Then from there, they send the information to the brain.

You caught the fish, but now it's time to remove the hook from its mouth. Trying to unhook a squirming fish can lead to getting poked and even cutting yourself if you're not careful.

harmed by your hook if you aren't careful when you are casting. According to the Hunting and Fishing section of *The Weather Channel*'s Web site, fishers should:

- Make sure to look around when casting so your hook does not hit a power line, tree, or another person;

- Never leave tackle lying on the ground so others won't trip over it or step on it;

- Never put your hand deep inside a fish's mouth to remove a hook. Use pliers instead;

Fishing hooks might be hard to see, especially if they are lying out on top of a dock. Put everything you are not using away so no one accidentally steps on it and gets hurt.

- Always remove hooks and lures from your line and store them in a tackle box when transporting equipment.

Life jackets are important even if not fishing on a boat. Always expect the unexpected.

WATER SAFETY

The same general water-safety rules that apply anytime you are around water also apply to fishing expeditions. Personal flotation devices (life jackets) are a must, even if you are not planning to be on a boat or even go in the water at all. It is also recommended that you always fish with a partner, never run around water, and know how to swim before you go fishing.

   If someone you are with does fall into the water and begins to struggle, you will need to know what to do. It is best to try to save them by means other than diving in after them. Many experts preach what is called the "Reach-Throw-Row-Go" method of saving someone struggling in the water.

First, you should reach out to the person from the shore with your arm, boat oar, or even your fishing pole. Throwing something that floats to the person is the next option. If that doesn't work—and you're in a boat or there is one nearby—row to the person and try to get them to grab onto the side of the boat, or reach for them if they can't do so. Only go in the water yourself to try to save the person as a last resort, and only if you are a good swimmer and have been trained in saving others. People who are drowning often panic and can endanger the life of the person trying to save them.

WHAT TO WEAR

Dressing for success isn't a slogan that only applies to the working world. It also applies to those who go fishing. Hats protect you from the sun, and keep your head dry and warm. Shoes are vital for a variety of reasons, and glasses will protect your vulnerable eyes from the sun—and from any stray hooks if you or someone you are fishing with happens to make an errant cast.

It also is important to be prepared for different types of weather. Sunscreen is important, even on cloudy days. Even if the forecast calls for clear skies and moderate temperatures, leaving the house with only shorts and a T-shirt is not advisable. Weather conditions can quickly change, so wearing layers that you can remove or add as needed or placing some extra clothes in a backpack before you leave the house is important to do. Just don't forget to pack it in the car!

First-aid kits, food and beverages, insect repellent, and waterproof wading boots are just some of the other fishing supplies you may wish to bring along with you on your freshwater fishing adventure.

ETIQUETTE

During periods of the year when fish are plentiful, it is likely you will have to share even what you believed to be *your* private fishing spot with one or several other people. It is not uncommon to see people fishing elbow-to-elbow at some popular spots located near big cities. If you find yourself fishing in a not-so-solitary location, knowing what is considered to be good manners in the fishing world can help everyone avoid a headache.

Some people like to yell "fish on" when they have hooked a fish. This helps alert other fishers that you may be moving from the position you are in—and may cross over into the area where they are standing—in an attempt to land your fish. In most instances, other fishers will be courteous and will reel their lines in while you battle your fish so your lines don't cross and tangle.

Being quiet and considerate of others also is important part of fishing etiquette. Loud music, yelling, and sudden loud noises, especially rustling in the water, can spook fish and send them swimming away to other parts of the lake or river, never to been seen again. Never wade out into the water in front of a fellow angler, and never leave unused bait or trash by the water when you leave.

ICE FISHING

Unless you live in areas where frozen bodies of water are the norm, chances are you can use a few tips on how to take part in a unique type of fishing called ice fishing. In general, ice fishing involves fishing through holes in frozen lakes, streams, or rivers. Knowing what ice you can safely walk on—and what ice you can't—is important when ice fishing. "There is no such thing as 100 percent safe ice," says the Minnesota Department of Natural Resources. The agency does, however, provide some tips on its Web site that can increase the odds of having a safe ice-fishing adventure. Those tips include knowing that:

- New ice is stronger than old ice.
- Ice seldom freezes uniformly. Ice that's too thin to support a child may be located just inches away from a section of ice that's thick enough to hold several adults.
- Ice formed over flowing water and currents is often dangerous.
- Booming and cracking ice isn't necessarily dangerous.
- Ice near the shore can be weaker than ice that is farther out.

Once you've determined where you want to fish, when you can do it, and what gear you're going to use, you're finally ready to hit the water. Of course, all the pre-planning and fancy gear in the world isn't going to help if you don't know how to actually *fish*.

Ice fishing takes special skill and determination. It is a constant battle against the freezing temperatures.

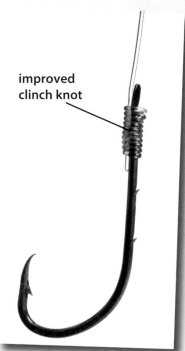

HOW TO FISH

So how do you fish? Fishing is a skill that is often passed down by example from generation to generation. Showing someone how to fish is a lot easier than telling them how to do it. Still, there are many fishing basics you can learn about simply by reading about them.

TYING KNOTS

As any good Boy Scout or Girl Scout will tell you, there are several ways to tie a knot. Once you have arrived at your fishing spot (your rod and reel should be preassembled), your knot-tying skills will take center stage so you can affix whatever terminal tackle you plan to use to the end of your line.

improved clinch knot

The most popular knot used for freshwater fishing is called the improved clinch knot. It involves threading your line through your terminal tackle (swivel, lure, hook, sinker, etc.), twisting the line several

The improved clinch knot is very helpful when threading your line through your fish hook.

times, threading it back through the lowest loop, and then pulling it tight.

Other common knots include the Palomar knot, the loop knot, the king sling knot, the double clinch knot, and the hangman's knot.

BAITING A HOOK

Earthworms are the most common bait used in freshwater fishing because they are easy (yet somewhat yucky) to handle and most fish like to eat them.

To fish with earthworms, you will first need to collect some from your yard, compost pile, or buy some from a store. If you are fishing for smaller fish, you can cut the worms into pieces and thread several of those pieces onto your hook until it is completely covered. Fish may not be the smartest creatures on the planet but they know their surroundings well enough to know that a piece of shiny metal doesn't belong and isn't edible.

If you'd rather use a whole worm, the process is similar. In that case, you slide your hook through the worm's body, then fold the worm over and slide it onto the hook again. Repeat the process until the worm is securely attached to the hook and the hook is covered.

The procedure is identical if you're using live maggots as bait. Hooking live crickets and minnows is a bit more complicated, but easily achievable with a little practice.

ATTACHING A LURE

Those who squirm at the thought of using squishy worms, maggots—or any type of live bait—on their hook have many options. Those options are called lures. Lures are artificial devices meant to attract, or lure, fish to bite. Lures tie directly to the end of your line, and work their way through the water either by you lifting and lowering your pole, by reeling in your line, or both. Lures can be as basic as plastic earthworms, or as complicated as spinnerbaits, which combine the benefits of spinners and baits into one lure.

CASTING/REELING

Casting and reeling take some practice to master. Fortunately, you do not need to be near a water source to practice. Those techniques can be practiced in your backyard by tying any number of objects onto the end of your line (leave the hooks off when you're practicing) and then going for it until you've got the process down.

The type of bait you use will help determine exactly where in the water you should cast your line and also how you should reel it in once you've cast. When using worms, for example, you oftentimes can simply cast your line out into the water and wait for a fish to bite before you need to take any further action. When using spoons or jigs, there will be no resting because you will constantly be using your pole and reel to make the lures move.

SENSING BITES AND SETTING HOOKS

How do you know if a fish has taken your bait? Basically, it is when you detect any movement in your lure, line, or at the top of your pole that feels different from what it does when a fish isn't biting your line. Sometimes, a bite will be obvious and you will notice a large movement. Other times, the bite will be small and hardly noticeable. Using bobbers that float on top of the water and create ripples when bites occur are typically thought to be the easiest way for beginners to know if they have a fish on.

Once you have detected a bite, you will need to plant your hook securely into the fish's mouth. This is called "setting the hook." You set the hook by jerking the top of your rod back after you feel the bite.

PLAYING A FISH

Your adrenaline will be flowing when you hook a fish. Especially your first one. When that moment arrives, your natural reaction may be to reel in your line as quickly as possible. In most instances, that would be a mistake. By reeling in quickly, you can yank the hook right out of the fish's mouth and lose your prey.

Instead, you need to do what is called "playing" the fish. The idea is to let the fish swim around and fight for a while until it is tired out. At that point, you can reel in the fish without a struggle. Playing a fish involves mastering several features of your reel, including the drag. The drag is the part of your reel that controls how easy or difficult it is to pull out line. You will want the fish to be able to pull out some line while you are playing it.

LANDING A FISH

Once the fish is tired and you've got it close to shore, it is time to land it. Doing this involves using a net, and placing the net in the water under the fish. Once the net is under the fish, you simply use it to lift the fish out of the water.

NOW WHAT?

Long before you left on your fishing adventure you should have made an important decision: Am I going to release what I catch or am I going to keep it? The answer to that question will help dictate the gear you use,

Earthworms are by far the most common bait used when freshwater fishing and can usually be found in the yard.

Fishing lures come in all different sizes, colors, and shapes.

especially the type of hook and bait. Those planning to release their catch are better off using barbless hooks and artificial bait, which lessens the chance of a fish swallowing the tackle. Once a fish has swallowed a hook, it is extremely difficult to remove the hook without seriously injuring the fish.

It is best to land a fish as quickly as possible, and keep it in the water while you remove the hook if you plan to release it. Once the hook is removed, gently hold the fish and move it back and forth a few times before letting it swim away by itself.

Those who plan to keep their catch must first determine if it is a legal catch. Exactly what constitutes "legal" varies from area to area, so you will need to consult with others or a fisheries department to see what that is in your area. If it is legal to keep your fish, you will need to decide which technique you want to use. Some experts believe in using a stringer to tie the fish they catch together to keep them alive throughout the day. After stringing the fish, they keep the fish in the water until they are ready to go home.

Other experts say it is best to kill the fish immediately by clubbing it on the head. After the clubbing, some anglers will "bleed" their catch by cutting it open in a specific way with a knife or scissors.

At some point before you cook it, you will need to clean your fish. According to the guidebook *Moon Washington Fishing*, the best way to do so is to:

- Slit the belly from anal vent to gills;

- Sever the lower junctions of the gills;

- Pull out the innards and gills;

- Run your thumbnail along the inner cavity to clean out all dark matter.

- Most people also cut the head and the tail off at some point. Once your fish is cleaned, all that is left is the cooking. That can be done in many ways, too. Regardless of which way you choose, one thing is certain: Fresh-caught fish—especially fish that was caught by *you*—tastes extra good.

STORING YOUR GEAR

You've been fishing all afternoon in the heat. You're tired and hungry. You've caught your fish and you want to hurry home to fry it (or them) up in a pan with butter. Many an angler faced with similar circumstances has thrown common sense to the wind, quickly tossed their pole into the car, and drove for home. This is a good way to damage, or even break, your pole. Make sure you store your pole in a secure place (floating freely in the back of a pickup truck is not a secure place) before you hit the road. Gear used in saltwater fishing trips should be cleaned after each use due to the damage saltwater can cause. Non-salty freshwater isn't as hard on equipment, thus fishing gear used in freshwater doesn't need as much care.

Seeing how far you can cast can be fun to do, but only if it can be done in a controlled manner.

DID YOU KNOW?

According to the American Sportfishing Association, more than 46 million Americans fish at least one time each year. Each year, that number continues to grow. There is no single, simple answer as to why that is the case.

When the fishing season is over for the year, though, you will need to spend some time caring for your gear so it will be ready—and working—for you when the next season rolls around. The *Take Me Fishing* Web site suggests doing the following before storing your gear for long periods of time:

- Take your reels apart and clean, grease, and oil them;
- Check for loose guides and wraps and repair or replace if any issues are found;
- Store rods vertically so they don't develop a permanent bend;
- Examine your line for wear and replace if necessary;
- Replace or sharpen rusty or bent hooks;
- Replace all broken lures and any missing tools.

Each person who fishes does so for his or her own reasons. Some fish because they enjoy adventuring alone. Others fish as a means of socializing with friends or family. Some enjoy the sound the water makes when a lure splashes into it. Others enjoy the times when there are no sounds at all. Fishing is a challenging sport, and one that our ancestors have been participating in for tens of thousands of years. In many ways it is natural and instinctual to fish. And those who fish once are often hooked for life.

FURTHER READING

BOOKS

Carpenter, Tom. *Freshwater Fishing: Bass, Trout, Walleye, Catfish, and More*. Minneapolis, Minn.: Lerner Publishing Group, 2012.

Dirks, David E. *Basic Illustrated Freshwater Fishing*. Enfield, CT: FalconGuides, 2014

Gilbey, Henry. *Boy Scouts of America's Be Prepared Fishing*. New York: DK CHILDREN, 2008.

Howard, Melanie A. *Freshwater Fishing for Kids*. North Mankato, Minn. Capstone Press, 2012.

Kaminsky, Peter and Greg Schwipps. *Fishing for Dummies*. New York: Wiley Publishing, Inc., 2011.

Seymour, Mike. *The Smart Guide to Freshwater Fishing*. Norman, Okla.: Smart Guide Publications, Inc., 2012.

INTERNET ADDRESSES

Fishing in Freshwater
<http://www.howtofishguide.com/freshwater-fishing.html>

Freshwater Fishing, Angling Tips And Techniques
<http://www.fishingloft.com/>

What is Freshwater Fishing, Freshwater Fishing Tips
<http://takemefishing.org/fishing/freshwater-fishing/what-is-freshwater-fishing/>

INDEX